STANLEY GIBBONS GUIDES

STAMP VARIETIES EXPLAINED

James Watson

STANLEY GIBBONS PUBLICATIONS LTD

391 Strand, London WC2R 0LX

By Appointment to Her Majesty The Queen
Stanley Gibbons Ltd, London
Philatelists

© Stanley Gibbons Publications Ltd 1978

First published 1978

ISBN 0 85259 041 5

Set in 8 on 9pt Monotype Century Schoolbook and
printed in Great Britain by Waterlow (Dunstable) Ltd

The Author

James Watson, well-known stamp journalist, writer and lecturer, was born and educated in Clifton, Bristol, and now lives in Stanmore, Middlesex. He joined Stanley Gibbons in 1946 after wartime army service in Aldershot and Nairobi, East Africa, and became a member of the editorial team of Gibbons *Stamp Monthly* in 1952.

Since that time he has contributed regular features to the magazine, including the popular varieties series, 'Through the Magnifying Glass', which he took over in September 1968, and he is particularly interested in stamp design and printing.

Mr. Watson is the author of numerous stamp books and guides, and of an authoritative handbook on modern 8 mm cine-photography. Appointed deputy editor of *Stamp Monthly* in 1972, he is now in semi-retirement as the magazine's associate editor. He is an avid collector of old picture postcards, especially those reflecting the life and times of the Edwardian era.

Contents

Illustrations: The illustrations of varieties in this Guide have been enlarged by differing amounts and do not reflect the comparative size of the original stamps. The illustrations on pages 5, 6, 23 and 29 showing various aspects of stamp printing are reproduced by courtesy of The Post Office.

1. Introduction

The stamp collector is an odd creature! Philately is probably the only field in the whole range of collectable printed matter and ephemera where the imperfect article is often more eagerly sought than the normal, 'perfect' one. Errors and flaws on stamps have existed ever since the Penny Black and Twopence Blue were issued by Great Britain in 1840, and they are attractive to many collectors. They extend the horizons of the ordinary collector, provide a secondary interest to the specialist and, in many instances, have a calculable scarcity value. The thrill of the hunt may be more than equalled by the discovery of an important and worthwhile variety.

This little guide aims to introduce all the different kinds of stamp variety in as simple and straightforward a manner as possible, providing both embryo and established collectors with concise descriptions of the basic types of variety allied to each of the different printing processes, explaining how they are caused and how they can be identified and located. It is important to be able to sort the wheat from the chaff, to discriminate and to assess the comparative interest of a specific item among the innumerable dots and dashes prevalent on modern stamps. Many minor flaws have no especial significance and, to avoid time-wasting forays and searches, their characteristics also are described in the text.

Generally, preference is given to varieties which are patently abnormal and visible to the naked eye. They should be constant – that is, recurring in at least part of a printing run – and their position in a sheet of stamps should be located and recorded for the benefit of other collectors, also for possible catalogue listing. The sheet position is indicated by a simple formula according to which horizontal row contains a specific stamp. If it is the third from the left in the sixth row down, for example, this would be shown as R.6/3, that is, row 6, stamp 3.

British stamps are the 'happy hunting ground' for collectors of varieties, but of course the stamps of the whole world are printed by one or other of the processes described, and may be equally rewarding to study. Fortuitous mishaps such as paper creases and folds, and other 'once only' abnormalities are not included in the text.

G.B. and Commonwealth varieties are listed in the Gibbons *British Commonwealth* and *Elizabethan Specialised* catalogues, while the ultimate in reference works for the dedicated G.B. collector is the Gibbons *Great Britain Specialised* catalogue in four volumes. The Gibbons *Europe* and *Overseas* catalogues record major varieties.

Stamp varieties make an unusual and exciting sideline collection, and it is hoped that this book will encourage and help collectors to find new and interesting ones.

J.W.

2. Printing Varieties

Line-engraved (Recess-printed) stamps

An engraved stamp is easily identified: the printed design stands up on the surface of the paper and you can feel the raised impression with your finger. That's the first step in seeking stamp varieties: establishing the method of printing and production. Knowledge of the process will assist you in finding the particular types of flaw allied to it, and each process has its own characteristics and peculiarities.

Line-engraving is the oldest and most respected method of printing postage stamps.

It was the virtual monopoly of the steel-engraving process which enabled Perkins, Bacon and Petch (later Perkins, Bacon and Co.) to secure the contract for printing the world's first postage stamps. The inventions of Jacob Perkins of Massachusetts, notably the capability of softening and hardening steel and the introduction of the transfer roller, made possible the mass production of the line-engraved Penny Blacks and Twopence Blues in 1840.

The process is described in some detail here because some of the most important varieties have occurred in the middle stage of manufacture, the operation of the transfer roller. The stamp design is incised or cut on a small plaque of steel by the engraver, in recess (hence 'recess-printing') and in reverse. The *master die* (as this plaque is called) is then hardened and the design image applied under pressure to the curved surface of the transfer roller, a cylinder of softened steel.

The surface of the roller, which now bears the design image as a raised right-reading impression (not in reverse), is next hardened and the design again transferred, as often as required to form a sheet of stamps, to the softened steel plate which will be eventually used to print them. This procedure is known as 'rocking in' and each impression on the plate is literally rocked in with a single to and fro movement. In days of yore the roller operator had to rock in 240 separate images to form a sheet of stamps. He had only the guide lines and dots on the virgin plate to assist him in the alignment of twenty rows of twelve stamps.

The *re-entry* is one of the most notable varieties on recess-printed stamps. This term popularly covers three distinct types of variety, but strictly speaking it applies only to instances where a plate was used for printing and, having been subjected to wear or damage, had its faulty section re-entered, causing visible duplication if the design images did not exactly correspond. Failure of the return run of the transfer roller to coincide with the outward run is termed a

Here the design image is impressed onto the transfer roller from the master die.

shifted transfer. When a faint impression was rocked in a second time or when a badly misaligned image was burnished out and an entirely new impression transferred by the roller the term *fresh entry* is used. Re-entries, shifts and fresh entries are visible in the printed stamps as doubling of portions of the design or lettering. So now we come to plate-making and the prospect of more varieties!

It would be no exaggeration to say that a completed plate of the first 1d. and 2d. stamp impressions would contain a host of imperfections: traces of the guidelines and dots, rough edges formed by the so-called 'burrs' or ridges of metal displaced during the rocking in, and weak impressions due to inadequate pressure by the roller. It was the engraver's job to remove these blemishes while the plate was still soft, prior to being hardened and made ready for the press.

The fact that numerous varieties exist on the issued stamps (examples follow) is no reflection on the engraver; often the guidelines and dots and other flaws were in inaccessible places on the designs and could not be removed without causing further damage. Weak, shallow entries were deepened by the engraver with his burin or graver, and these *retouches* (as they are called) appear as an intensification of colour and engraving on parts of the stamp design.

The 1d. blacks (and 1d. reds of 1841) and 2d. blues had letters in the lower corner squares as a precaution against forgery, and these were punched onto the plate by hand. Each horizontal row had a different combination of letters, starting with AA, AB, AC etc. in row one, and there were four 'alphabets' or styles of letters, three of them hand-punched, the fourth hand-engraved. Again, numerous varieties of the corner letters have been recorded, for example misshapen letters and double impressions caused when an original misplaced letter was insufficiently erased or when a punch jumped in the striker's hand.

Printing the early line-engraved stamps was a laborious process. The hand-made stamp paper had first to be dampened, sometimes causing uneven expansion and contraction of a sheet of stamps, while the printing ink was dabbed on to the plate by hand to fill the recessed lines. The surplus ink was wiped off and the plate polished (with the palm of the hand!) before paper and plate were brought together in the flat-bed

The design image is rocked onto the printing plate, repeated as many times as is necessary to fill a sheet or pane.

Major re-entry at upper right on the G.B. 2s. 6d. 'Seahorse' printed by Bradbury, Wilkinson.

Re-entry on and above diadem on stamp R.8/1 of the 5s. G.B. 'Castle' issue, Waterlow printing.

S.G. 272a of Australia, a clear re-entry on the 3½d. Royal Visit stamp issued in 1954.

Re-entry on stamp R. 10/1, the 1957 Australia 3½d. Christmas stamp, S.G. 298a.

press, and the process repeated, sheet by sheet.

Varieties in the actual printing were surprisingly few, and were due mainly to scratches and wear on the plates: any kind of indentation would show as an extraneous coloured mark on the stamp, while any foreign matter adhering to the surface of the plate (that is, the recessed portion) would appear as a white blob on the coloured stamp. Stamps printed from worn plates show a deterioration and blurring of the fine detail. A good example is the 1d. grey-black (S.G. 3).

The 1d. black was printed from eleven plates (twelve if one includes plate 1b, the repaired version of plate 1). Two of them were adapted to print the first 2d. blue stamps, while the first printings of the 1d. red were made from seven of the 'black' plates. Each plate of 240 impressions has its characteristic varieties and corner letters which, when the stamps are reassembled in their correct sheet sequence, make possible (in theory at least but an expensive proposition these days!) the reconstruction of an original sheet, known to philatelists as *plating*. Almost 300 plates were used to print the first-type 1d. reds.

**The 1935 Jubilee 'Extra Flagstaff' variety: an enlargement (left)
and on the upper left stamp of a positional block (right)**

The early line-engraved issues provide unlimited scope for the variety collector. Each plate had its crop of flaws: re-entries, double letters in the corners and guidelines through corners and values. The stars in the upper corners are of interest, not only as an aid to identifying the different plates, but also as flaws in themselves. The well-known double star, called the 'Union Jack' re-entry because of its resemblance to the flag, occurs on a 1d. red (plate 75). The normal star has twelve rays or points, and these may be found in shortened form or entirely missing. Their location is indicated as at '7 o'clock' or, say, '10 o'clock' on the star.

Corner letters were frequently malformed. The best known of these is probably the 'J' flaw which occurred on the earlier plates, a square-footed 'J' caused by a faulty punch. On one of the 'black' plates (10) and on several of the 'red' plates the letter 'R' is formed from the letter 'P', the tail being hand cut. And the corner letter 'S' is commonly found inverted (with the larger loop at the top) on the original 1d. red-brown stamps. The error ÓP-PC for CP-PC occurs on the 1½d. of 1870.

The perforated 1d. reds of 1858-79 (with letters in all four corners) introduced plate numbers, ranging from Nos. 71 to 225, inserted in tiny figures in the trellis of the side borders, and again there are numerous examples of malformed or misplaced figures to engage our attention. These small white plate numbers were engraved on the transfer roller, and seven plates (Nos. 7 to 9 and 12 to 15) were similarly inscribed for the perforated 2d. blue stamps.

Recess-printed stamps were reintroduced in Britain in 1913. These were the popular high-value 'Seahorses', designed by Bertram Mackennal, engraved by J.A.C. Harrison and printed successively by Waterlow Bros. & Layton, De La Rue (1915) and Bradbury, Wilkinson (1918). There were several well-defined re-entries, mostly on the 2s. 6d. value

**Tail to 'N' on the G.B. 1924 1d.
'Wembley' commemorative.**

and usually confined to Britannia's shield and the frame-lines. A major re-entry or group of re-entries occurred on the B.W. 2s. 6d., involving almost the entire design. The stamp is R.1/2 in the sheet.

Fortuitous gashes and lines on the printing plate appear in the colour of the issued stamp, and an example of this may be seen on one of the British Empire Exhibition (Wembley) 1d. scarlet stamps of 1924 on which the 'N' of EXHIBITION has a curved 'tail'. The King George VI high values of 1939-48 had numerous re-entries and flaws, notably on the shield of the 2s.6d. green and 5s. red, and on the scroll below the King's portrait on the 10s. dark blue. The £1 brown of 1951 shows a re-entry in the word DIEU below the Arms.

The 'Castle' high values of 1955-58 have some minor flaws, while a major re-entry on the 5s. (Waterlow printing) first came to light in 'Through the Magnifying Glass' (*Gibbons Stamp Monthly*, vol. 41, p. 49, November 1967); it is R.8/1 in the sheet and consists of double vertical lines of background above the Queen's diadem and along the edges of the crosses. The recess-printed 'Machin' high values, now obsolete, may be found with minor flaws, breaks and scratches. The 2s.6d. is known with an 'accent' over the '6'.

Until recent times it was not possible to print bi-coloured or multicoloured stamps by recess in one motion through the press.

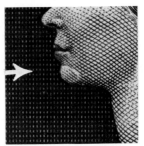

Scar on the Queen's chin on the 50p G.B. Machin definitive.

Separate plates were made for the *vignette* or centre design and for the frame. The vignette was usually shaded off at the edges to minimise the effects of mis-registration when first the frame and then the vignette (or vice versa) were printed. But there were numerous instances of poor registration with the vignette impinging on one side or the other of the frame, leaving a wide gap on the opposite side. These are loosely termed colour shifts although in effect they are design shifts.

Examples may be found among the bi-coloured line-engraved stamps of British Guiana (Jubilee, 1898), Ceylon (1935-36, 1938-49, etc.), Cyprus (1934, 1938-51, etc.), Jamaica (1919-21, 1921-29, etc.) and Kenya, Uganda and Tanganyika (1935-36, 1938-54, etc.). Shifts do not have very great significance as varieties, but there is always the chance of making an

Three recess varieties: left, 'beauty spot' on Queen Victoria's chin on Canada S.G. 907, the 1978 'Capex' issue; centre, flaw in frame of G.B. 10s. 'Seahorse'; right, accent over '6' on the 1969 G.B. 2s.6d. Machin (S.G. 787).

9

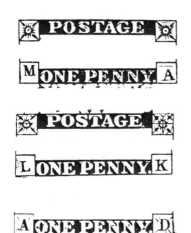

Three re-entries on the line-engraved 1d. red of Great Britain. Top, stamp MA, Die I, Plate 39. Centre, the 'Union Jack' re-entry, stamp LK, Die I, Plate 75. Bottom, doubling between stamps AD and BD, Die II, Plate 27.

exciting discovery – an inverted vignette or frame! Instances include the Canada 5c. St Lawrence Seaway (1959), Cook Islands 1d. (1932), Jamaica 1s. (1920) and Kenya, Uganda and Tanganyika 5c. of 1954 (only one known).

These exceptional errors were caused when a single sheet of partly printed stamps was fed into the press for the second printing, either of the vignette or the frame, wrong way round. But a quite extraordinary variation on this theme occurred with the printing by De La Rue of the Falkland Islands 'Battle' stamps of 1964: the vignette of the 6d. stamp, which normally showed H.M.S. *Kent*, was discovered with the picture of H.M.S. *Glasgow*, which belonged to the 2½d. denomination!

Some good re-entries are to be found on Australian stamps: the 1½d. 'Swan' (1929), 6d. 'Kingsford Smith' (1931), 3½d. 'Royal Visit' (1954) and 3½d. 'Christmas' (1957), while the 'Navigators' of 1963-65 and 1966-71 are turning up with weak entries and broken frame-lines. An interesting example of re-engraving is recorded in the appropriate catalogues in relation to the 6c. definitive in the Canadian 1967-72 series. The original die was duplicated by transfer, and later the duplicate die was re-engraved to make fresh plates. The different versions show marked contrasts. Ireland's 3½p 'Rugger' stamp of 1974 showed a clear re-entry – doubled frame-lines and inscriptions – on R.4/1 of certain panes.

The Bradbury, Wilkinson printings of the King George V Silver Jubilee omnibus series for the Bechuanaland Protectorate, Gambia, Sierra Leone and other Commonwealth countries included the constant 'Extra Flagstaff' variety on all four values printed from the vignette plate – a chance plate scratch.

While the British Post Office has finally abandoned line-engraved stamps for its definitive high values, other countries, notably France and Sweden, continue to employ recess processes, using modern and sophisticated multicolour techniques, often combined with the photogravure or lithography processes.

Britain's first recess-and-photo stamps, the 'Sailing' issue of 1975, had a rough passage, partly through a labour dispute. Very many flaws occurred among the outlines, waves and rigging recess-printed in black.

Typographed (Letterpress-printed) stamps

'Typography' in its literal meaning is simply the art or style of printing, particularly those branches of it concerned with the designing, setting and arrangement of type. 'Letterpress' is primarily a printer's term for printed matter, and both words have been adapted to identify stamps printed from raised type, where the design image stands in relief on the plate, also known as 'surface-printing'.

The traditional method of printing stamps by typography, as introduced by De La Rue for British stamps in 1855, was virtually the opposite in principle to line-engraving. The master die was cut in reverse (and in relief) on steel by the engraver, the unwanted portions of the design being cut away. Then duplicate impressions, as many as required to form a printing plate of, say, sixty stamps, were made by transfer under pressure to stamp-size lead moulds. These were clamped together in a chase or frame and immersed in a vat where, by the process of *electrotyping*, a copper shell was formed on the moulds.

The copper shell, comprising exact replicas of the original die, was backed with a metal alloy (consisting mainly of lead) and prepared for use as the printing plate. The surface of the plate was coated with nickel or steel (in modern times chromium is used) for prolonged life. A similar and cheaper process, *stereotyping*, using plaster of Paris moulds and metal alloy castings was sometimes used. The Cape of Good Hope so-called 'Woodblock' provisionals were printed from stereotyped plates.

Typographed stamps are printed from the raised portions of the plate which are inked and transferred directly to the paper in the press. They are usually distinguishable from other kinds of surface-printed stamps by visible traces of the impression – ink squeezed out from parts of the design, especially the corners of ruled frames, and perhaps the outline of the design showing in relief on the back. Defects which may eventually appear as philatelic varieties may occur at any stage of electrotyping or plate-making, but the most common cause of typo flaws and broken letters etc. in stereotyped overprints is plate damage, to which raised type is especially prone.

De La Rue's first stamp in the long series of G.B. surface-printed issues was the 4d. carmine of 1855-7; a typical break in the frame of the rose or rose-carmine version was

Top, white dots added to Q.V. typographed 3d., and, bottom, hair lines in corner of Q.V. 4d., 6d. and 9d.

recorded in 'Through the Magnifying Glass' (*Stamp Monthly*, vol. 1, p. 257, March 1971). An interesting variety is the 'K in circle' on the 1s. green of 1862 with corner letters 'K' and 'D' (S.G. 90a): the corner letters were repaired by plugs and in this instance the 'K' plug was not sufficiently driven home, making a circular indentation on the stamp.

The 6d. chestnut of 1872 (S.G. 122/3) has plate numbers in the lower corners and is known with the figure '11' damaged (it has long, drooping serifs), while the 6d. buff stamp (S.G. 124) and the 6d. grey (of 1873, S.G. 125) may be found with the figure '12' doubled.

Some additions and alterations to the printing plate were made for a specific purpose and, though interesting, are not varieties in the unpremeditated sense. Plate 3 of the 3d. rose of 1862 was identified by two dots placed in the frame flanking the Queen's portrait, almost level with her chin. The plate was rejected after a small trial printing, and the 'dotted' stamp is a rarity. The 4d., 6d. and 9d. values of the 1862-64 series exist with fine hair-lines across the lettered corners. These distinguished subsequent plates and the 9d. (plate 3) is the rare one. The 6d. mauve of 1869-70 without a hyphen between SIX and PENCE (plates 8, 9 and 10) was a deliberate amendment.

The well-known LH-FL (for LH-HL) error in the corner letters of the 2½d. rosy mauve, plate 2, of 1875 was simply due to the wrong letter being struck but it was not discovered until some years after its issue.

The charming little 1d. lilac stamp of 1881, which first had 14 corner dots or 'pearls' but was replaced by the 16-dot version after a few months, was used for more than 20 years, and, not surprisingly, acquired numerous varieties and plate flaws during that time. Two major frame breaks are

'Squashed dots' on lower left-hand corner of G.B. 1d. lilac.

recorded, other minor breaks exist and all were caused by plate damage. 'White' flaws, such as a serif on the 'I' of INLAND, were the result of cuts and scratches on the plate, while fortuitous blobs and streaks of colour or solid colour instead of lines of shading were invariably due to clogging of the raised type. The stamp is known printed on the gummed side or on both sides.

The 'Jubilee' issue of 1887-1900 introduced Britain's first bi-coloured stamps, the Queen's head and parts of the surround or frame being printed from 'Head' plates, and the value tablets or frames and tablets (in the second colour) from 'Duty' plates. Registration was good with only minor variations or shifts of the value tablet, mostly on the 2d. and 5d. values. The numerous varieties on all values – frame breaks, deformed letters and emblems, and extraneous dots and blemishes – can be attributed to flaws on the printing plates.

Some plates developed minor (hairline) cracks during use and these are visible on some stamps, notably the ½d. vermilion, as fine white lines. The 1½d. has a constant variety, the 'horns' on top of the two figures '1' in '1½d', while the 2d. is known with a double frame-line on the left of the design. A damaged matrix was probably the cause of the 'shading omitted' within the figure '4' on the 4d. (in some instances this occurs in all four corner numerals). The 4½d. is found with a dot between the '4' and '½', or as a full stop under the 'd', while on the 5d. the second lion in the upper left corner of the shield has a broken leg – its paw is detached!

Certain values of the Edwardian issues of 1901-10 repeated the 'Jubilee' designs and similar flaws are found on them. Damage to frames and value tablets is fairly common, as also are the repairs to individual clichés on the plate by the insertion of 'plugs' of metal to replace damaged parts of the design. These are visible as small white rings on the stamp.

Typographed G.B. issues continued with the ½d. and 1d. stamps of King George V,

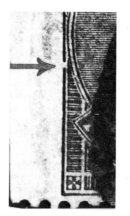

Two typical typo flaws: left, frame-break on 1855-57 4d.; right, white ring by plate number on 1s. of 1862.

'G' for 'C' in 'HALFPENCE' on the Great Britain 1½d. King George V definitive.

1911-12, but the first issue was of poor quality despite the making of fresh plates from a deepened die (Die B). A new and improved die was prepared; new stamps were printed and were issued on 1 January 1912. Varieties in the first issue included a cracked plate (a diagonal stroke across the 'F' of HALFPENNY), and a gash in the crown, on the ½d., and the well-known 'No cross on crown' on the 1d. The latter also occurred on the ½d, and 1d. of the three different watermarked issues of 1912. The cross on the crown jutted above the top frame-line and was vulnerable to damage, however the numerous faint impressions indicate that the missing crown was due to a plate weakness.

A new range of King George V stamps, showing the King's head in profile, began to be issued in the latter part of 1912 with the release of the 1d., 1½d., 2d., 2½d. and 3d. values. Flaws in the matrixes were responsible for the regular occurrence of the 'Q' for 'O' in ONE PENNY (also found reversed and inverted), and of the PENCF error on the 1½d. Broken and misshapen letters (e.g. 'G' for 'C') and frames are found on all values.

The last typographed stamps of the Georgian era were the four low values for the London U.P.U. Congress in 1929, the £1 stamp being recess-printed. They were printed by Waterlow from plates made at the Royal Mint and, apart from watermark variations, were 'clean' except for minor flaws. The 1½d. is known with '1829' for '1929'.

The Australian 'Kangaroo' and 'King's Head' stamps were typographed almost exclusively from the first issues of 1913 to about 1936. There were numerous changes of printer during that time, and some distinctive varieties are recorded. These include the retouched second 'E' in PENCE (6d. ultramarine of 1913), a line through FOUR PENCE (4d. orange of 1915 and 4d. violet of 1921 – a rare variety), and the well-known 'Leg of kangaroo broken' on the 6d. chestnut of 1923, which was inherited from the 6d. ultramarine of 1921.

White patches on the 1d. carmine-red (1914) were caused by rusting of the steel plate, and the substitute clichés (the units forming the plate) were distinguished by rounded corners and a weakness or omission of the top of the crown (compare the G.B. ½d. and 1d. 'No cross on crown' varieties of 1912). Thin figures in fractions and the interesting FOUR PENCE in thinner letters (4d. violet and 4d. ultramarine of 1921-22) were direct results of repairs to the defective cliche with line through FOUR PENCE mentioned above. Numerous minor flaws, malformed letters and ornaments, spots and blemishes occurred on these fascinating, but rather complex, issues.

All Hong Kong's definitive stamps up to 1960 – almost a hundred years from 1862! – were typographed by De La Rue and, apart from the surcharged issues of 1876-98, the various series were remarkably free from error. The King George V 25c. value of 1914 had a misformed Chinese character (the figure '2') at the top of the left-hand panel, due to an impediment on the plate, which was later rectified. The 4c. of 1921 had a similar flaw.

Varieties of the early typographed issues of Jamaica include the so-called 'SER.ET' (for SERVIET) error on the Arms-type stamps of 1905-11, due to a defect in the electrotyped

'$' for 'S' in 'SHILLING' on the Jamaican Queen Victoria 1s. stamp.

plate. It occurred, once in each sheet, on all values of the 1903-04 issue (½d., 1d., 2½d. and 5d.) and on the ½d. and 5d. of the 1905-11 multiple watermark series. The 'dollar' variety of the Jamaican 1 shilling, '$' for 'S' in SHILLING, originated in the first issue of 1860 and was repeated almost *ad infinitum* through the various printings to 1910. It was caused by a double scratch on the plate which could have been very easily corrected.

Typographed overprints, including surcharges, are, by the nature of the methods used, a prolific source of errors, flaws and varieties. There is hardly a country in the world which has not, at one time or other, in emergency situations, resorted to overprinting existing stamps. In the early days only the large printing firms had the facilities for making stereotyped types from complete settings of individual type units. The smaller colonies and territories invariably entrusted the overprinting to local newspaper offices which had never previously handled quantities of sheets of stamps, let alone printed on them!

Loose type, mixed founts or typefaces, careless assembly and printing account for the many and diverse varieties to be found on overprinted stamps – 'Bpitish' for 'British', inverted or double surcharges, broken, inverted or missing figures, letters or rules, missing or misplaced stops, surcharges omitted – you'll find them all in the catalogues!

An interesting phase of De La Rue's Victorian typography, which was extended to the reigns of Edward VII and George V, was the 'Key-plate' system. Stamps were printed from two plates, the *key plate* (or *head plate* as it usually bore the head of the reigning sovereign) and the *duty plate*

An unfortunate kangaroo with a broken leg! Australia S.G. 38ba.

Doubling of 'SIX PENCE' on St. Christopher Queen Victoria 6d.

Constant flaw on a typographed surcharge, listed as S.G. 1144 V49 of New Zealand.

which comprised the name of the colony and the figures of value. Identical key plates could be used for several colonies with appropriate duty plates, effecting considerable economies. Flaws inherent in the key plates could thus appear on the stamps of several colonies.

In modern stamp printing typography has limited usage, but the process was used by Bradbury, Wilkinson to print (with litho) the G.B. 'Inigo Jones' issue of 1973 (the 5p is known with missing serif to the 'n' in 'designer') and in the same year (with recess) the Commonwealth Parliamentary Conference stamps. Typographed stamps are occasionally found among the modern issues of Germany, Russia and French Overseas Territories or independent African states. They are printed on multicolour rotary presses.

Typography (or flexography, a similar kind of typo process) was used as an alternative to photogravure in the application of phosphor bands (which activate automatic letter-facing and sorting) to the G.B. 'Wilding' definitive stamps in the 1960s. The typo bands are solid (not screened) and usually indent the paper. They are found on the $2\frac{1}{2}$d. (1 band) and $4\frac{1}{2}$d. of 1961, and the $\frac{1}{2}$d., 1d., $1\frac{1}{2}$d., 6d. and 1s.3d. of 1965. Varieties in the form of misplaced or omitted bands are fairly common. With a few exceptions, all the G.B. special issues from 'National Productivity Year' (1962) to the 'Forth Road Bridge' (1964) had typo phosphor bands.

Lithographed stamps

The invention of lithography, the process of engraving or drawing on stone to produce a surface from which multiple reproductions could be made, is attributed to Alois Senefelder, 1771-1834, of Munich. A playwright, he was seeking a cheap means of printing his plays when he discovered by chance that he could 'print' from a greasy impression on a close-textured form of limestone. Etching away the blank portions of the design and liberally dousing the stone with water, he found that the printing ink adhered only to the greased image. Furthermore, he was able to transfer an inked design on paper to the stone under pressure (the image being in reverse), the impression being so sharp and clear that, following the watering, inking and hardening procedures, he could print as many times as he wished from what was virtually a flat (unetched) surface.

The early stamps of several British colonies were printed from lithographic stones (or *plates*) composed of transfers – as many as required to form a sheet of stamps – taken from the original stone (or *die*). Among them were the locally-printed 4d. blue 'Swans' of Western Australia, and a long list of transfer varieties is recorded in the Gibbons *British Commonwealth* catalogue. Any flaws or scratches on the original die are transferred also, and become constant varieties, but most of those recorded were due to 'squashed' transfers which caused squeezed-down letters. The famous 'Inverted Swan' was in fact an inverted frame, transferred in error.

Modern photo-lithography (or 'offset') still employs the basic 'grease and water' principle, but it has become an extremely efficient and sophisticated process. Briefly, the original artwork or design is photographed and 'printed-down' on to a flexible zinc or aluminium plate which is wrapped around a cylinder. During printing the design is offset onto a rubber blanket or roller and then transferred to the surface of the paper.

The preparatory photography involves making a colour transparency of the original artwork, reduction and multiplication of the design, processing of the colour separations which form the separate printing plates, and the inclusion of the halftone screen to provide a range of tones for each colour. The plates, now in the form of cylinders, are arranged in tandem in the press and, after being wetted and inked, contribute their separate colour images to the paper (passing through the press in single sheets or as a continuous web), offset by the blanket.

The offset lithographic process can be identified by the honeycomb of variable-sized dots forming the colours on the printed stamp, easily distinguished through a magnifying glass. Varieties generally occur during the printing run and in its final stages, and they are mostly peculiar to the offset process and its unique 'flat' printing. Letters and figures (which do not require tonal graduation) are printed in 'solid line' and are not screened, so they appear sharp and clear, another clue to identify the printing process. Flaws and blemishes occurring on inscriptions are easily spotted.

In litho printing, the primary colours – magenta, cyan (a greenish blue) and yellow – when combined, provide all the colours and tones necessary for a multicoloured stamp, not forgetting the addition of a 'solid' black plate. Scratches or marks on the thin metal printing plates which indent the surface (and fail to make contact with the inking rollers), appear on the stamps as white flecks or streaks. Imperfect registration of the cylinders in the press (just one may be fractionally out of alignment with the others) will result in an overlap of certain colours forming the stamp design, another form of colour shift.

Conversely any impediment, for example particles of grit, on the printing cylinder will be transferred, via the blanket roller, to the printed stamp. An interesting example is the Isle of Man series of postage due stamps issued in 1975: each of the eight values may be found with a red dot in the margin above the crown at the top, occurring on one stamp in the sheet, R.3/1.

Broken letters and frame-breaks are perhaps the most common litho faults. Repairs are not generally possible once a plate or cylinder has been put to use, but there is a classic example of one on the Nigeria 6d. postage due stamp of 1961. The original printing on Script CA water-marked paper of 1959 had a complete break in the frame-line encompassing the figure

Line across wall on 4b. Gambia 'Radio Gambia' commemorative.

of value, just above the 'R' of NIGERIA, on stamp R.8/4 in the sheet. It was repaired with a thin line on the second issue on the Multiple FN watermarked paper. Incidentally the colours were changed, the repaired 6d. being in yellow instead of red-orange.

Sometimes the particles of dust and grit previously mentioned build up on the plate, forming a bump which prevents the ink from reaching the area – this appears on the stamp as a *ring flaw*, a dot surrounded by a white ring. Larger, more extended flaws, similarly fringed by white borders, are due to 'skinned ink' – the quick-drying ink forms a skin in the trough and particles reach the printing plate and become attached to it. Such varieties are usually transient, though they may occur on several consecutive sheets.

Blanket stretch accounts for the apparent doubling of parts of an offset-lithographed design. When the rubber blanket is new it tends to expand lengthwise on the roller under pressure from the plate and impression cylinders (the latter presses the paper against the blanket). Eventually the sequence of printing is perfectly synchronised, but the original (misplaced) impressions on the blanket take time to wear off and these are seen as shadow images or doubling on the stamps. An example is the Bermuda 3d 'Settlement' stamp of 1959 which is recorded with a 'blanket offset'. Litho colours are

Frame-line break on 6d. postage due, S.G. D4 V5 of Nigeria.

Five litho flaws, from left to right: East Africa S.G. 95 V9, two dots to left of 'AT' on 5s. Livingstone-Stanley stamp of 1971; comma in place of full stop, S.G. 285 V12 of St. Christopher, Nevis and Anguilla; spot inside 'C' on $\frac{1}{4}$c. Sooty Tern definitive of Turks and Caicos Islands; S.G. 498 V25 of Mauritius, blue flaw on 'U'; S.G. 348E V33 of Jamaica, serif on 'I'.

inconsistent and tend to become diluted after long printing runs.

Offset lithography is extensively used in printing British Commonwealth stamps and those of foreign countries. The British 'Post Office Technology' (1969) and 'Commonwealth Games' (1970) issues were lithographed by De La Rue. A special photo-litho process, employing finely graduated halftone screens and known as *Delacryl*, is used by De La Rue.

Stamps printed by Photogravure

It is a sign of the times that all British postage stamps – 'Machin' definitives (including the high values), special or commemorative stamps, 'country' or regional issues, and postage due stamps – are now printed by the photogravure process. It is a comparatively economical method of producing stamps in large quantities, being particularly suited to long printing runs and the mass-production of both monochrome and multicoloured stamps in today's giant presses. Modern British Commonwealth and foreign stamps are also printed mainly by the photogravure and offset lithography processes, although recess-printing is still a formidable contender.

The profusion of photogravure-printing varieties and flaws which give so much pleasure to the collectors of modern stamps must be regarded in its true perspective – these so-called 'flyspecks' of philately are the merest fraction of the output of the printers who produce millions of stamps day by day. Printing standards are high and the photogravure process is one involving the most complicated and exacting procedures.

As its name implies, photogravure is a combination of photography and 'gravure' or recess-printing. The design subject ('artwork') is photographed by a 'step-and-repeat' camera and the negative is processed to provide a series of small-size images (as many as needed to form a sheet of stamps) on to a glass plate, known as the *multi-positive plate*, which is approximately the size of a sheet or pane of stamps.

So far we already have some likely sources of varieties. Both negative and multipositive are carefully examined for flaws and blemishes which, if not noticed and corrected, may become progressively apparent in the later stages of production. The multipositive is next processed upon a carbon tissue which has a 'screened' surface, forming a grid patterned with tiny dots. These vary in size and intensity in relation to the tonal variations, highlights and depths, which occur on the multiple images.

The carbon tissue is now wrapped around a copper cylinder (the printing cylinder) which is then etched, leaving a pattern of hollows and recesses on the stamp images; the deepest etching will produce the most intense colour tones during printing. G.B. definitives are generally printed in double-pane sheets, hence a second tissue is applied to the cylinder, alongside the first, and etched. Inadequate bonding of the carbon tissue with the cylinder causes the patches of weak colour or 'white' and the consequent retouches seen on the stamps.

Finally, the marginal sheet markings: numbers, arrows, rules, boxed colour dabs (the so-called 'traffic lights' which show that the stamp colours have registered correctly), etc. are added to the cylinder which is then chromium-plated and made ready for printing. Several cylinders may be made from a single multipositive plate, and any flaws on the plate which have escaped attention and correction may, therefore, appear on more than one cylinder and possibly on different values. These are known as *multipositive flaws*.

Photogravure-printed stamps can be identified by the overall pattern of microscopic dots over the printed surface (except on the white inscriptions, figures of value etc.), and by the coarse impression of the design image, which appears to have corrugated edges when viewed through a magnifying glass.

The current G.B. 'Machin' definitives are printed from cylinders incorporating the 'marriage' of two multipositives, one for the Queen's head and background (the 'standard' head for all similar denominations), the other for the face value. Faulty registration results in the screening dots appearing on the white figures of value or in the stamp margins, while the phenomenon of 'floating values' – variations in the location of the face value in relation to the head, often on a single sheet – is due to inexact registration of the two multipositives.

The cylinder numbers, which are important in the charting and recording of varieties (termed 'cylinder varieties' when they occur during printing), usually appear in the lower left margin, the 'no dot' pane on the left and the 'dot' pane (on which a dot or stop follows the numeral) on the right. Thus, in addition to describing the position of a stamp in the sheet (as explained in the Introduction) it is usual to state the appropriate cylinder number (if known). A typical catalogue entry would be shown as 'Cyl. 10 no dot, R.6/3', i.e. the third stamp in the sixth row down in a sheet marked (cylinder) '10' no dot.

Sometimes it is difficult to explain the exact location of a flaw on a stamp and the *Thirkell* Position Finder is an essential aid in this respect. It is described in Chapter 4.

Retouches are probably the most interesting photogravure varieties. Cylinders are carefully inspected before printing commences and any major flaws which would appear as conspicuous streaks or patches on the printed stamps are made good. The consequent retouch is evident on the stamp as a cluster of coloured dots forming a distinguishable patch. Some retouches are small and not easily seen, others are massive and easily recognised; the retoucher uses a burin (engraving tool) to make minute, pin-point indentations on the faulty patch which will be inked in the course of printing.

Even more interesting are the flaws which pass unnoticed and appear on the printed stamps and which may, at a later stage, be retouched on the cylinder before it is used again, providing collectors with examples of the two states: before and after retouching.

Random white patches may occur on stamps during printing, due to various causes, one of which is a form of *dry printing*, when the ink thickens slightly in the trough and tends to strip off the stamps as they are printed. Similarly, foreign matter may adhere to the printing cylinder and appear as spots, blobs and dashes of colour on the stamps. Sometimes these extraneous dabs are given picturesque descriptions, such as 'Wart on nose' or 'Flying saucer'.

Surface damage – scratches and gashes – may be due to careless handling of stamps in circulation. Paper clips are a notorious source of damage which may be seen as a

Partially omitted light magenta colour on the G.B. 7½p 'Paintings' stamp of 1973 depicting 'Nelly O'Brien' by Reynolds.

Hand drawn inscription (top) on the 9p G.B. 'Trees' stamp.

Dot on globe (and retouched at right) on G.B. 2½d. U.P.U. stamp of 1949.

A typical doctor blade flaw on this 3d. 'Wilding' G.B. definitive.

Obstruction on line in front of the British High Speed Train.

Broken frame-line on the beautiful G.B. 13p 'Jane Austen' stamp.

An amusing variety caused by a colour shift on the photogravure-printed 20c. Turks and Caicos Islands 1972 Silver Wedding stamp.

thinning of the paper when the stamp is held up to the light.

The numerous white dots and flecks inherent in the photogravure process inevitably occur amongst the fine detail of certain stamps, notably the emblems surrounding the Queen's head on the G.B. 'Wilding' ½d., 1d., 1½d. and 2d. stamps of 1952 onwards; the Queen's jewellery – pearl earrings and necklace – on the 'Machin' definitives (also the diadem in both series); and on the 'country' or regional issues from 1971 the Scottish lion and the Welsh dragon especially. Such flaws augment the numerous design breaks and omissions which occur so frequently and which are often of a minor nature.

Fine lines and letters do not reproduce well by photogravure, and this is especially noticeable in certain issues, such as the 'British Paintings' issue of 1973, and the 'Roses' set of 1976, both of which employed a finely printed, cursive style of type in the inscriptions. The resulting faint impressions or joined letters are best ignored.

Similarly the tiny imprints recording the names of artists or printers at the foot of certain G.B. commemorative stamps are extremely fickle, sometimes faint or only partially printed and often having broken letters. In certain instances the imprints have been so weak that they have been engraved by hand on the cylinder – examples can be identified by the crude and uneven capital letters. The 9d. 'Aberfeldy Bridge' stamp of 1968 (S.G. 764) is known (and listed) with both imprints – 'HARRISON' and 'RESTALL' – on adjoining stamps (R.18/3 and 4) redrawn by hand. Broken imprints are also commonly found on the photogravure-printed stamps of South Africa.

Multicoloured stamps are printed from a 'bank' of cylinders, each registering a specific colour (which is also a part of the design image) as the paper (in sheets or as a continuous web) passes through the press. Missing colours occur when the press is gradually slowed down to a stop for adjustment or at the end of a run, and the pressure

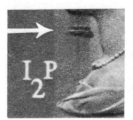

Left, 'blister' flaw on ½p G.B. Machin definitive. Right, broken '9' on 9p value of G.B. 'Paintings' series of 1973.

'Rosette' on lapel of composer Vaughan Williams (G.B. 1972 'Anniversaries').

on the printing cylinders is eased. A classic example is the missing Queen's head on the Great Britain 3d. 'National Productivity Year' stamp of 1962 (S.G. 632a): the sheet of stamps showed the light blue head progressively fading away.

Some missing colours are difficult to detect if they form a very small portion of the design or if they are laid on another colour or blended to create a third tone (for example the merging of blue and yellow to make green). Originally the small gold heads of the Queen which adorn G.B. special issues could be removed with a hard

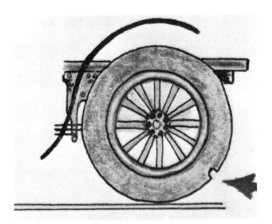

Large nick in tyre of British Fire Engine, the 3½p value of the 1974 series.

'Bullet holes' in Churchill's hat. One of the perils of being depicted on the 10p commemorative of 1974.

Left, blocked 'C' on the 8c. Trinidad and Tobago Royal Visit stamp of 1966. Right, this flaw retouched by the printer.

eraser (and a little patience!), making it difficult to identify genuine missing heads. The printers sought to rectify this by superimposing an embossed gold head over the flat-printed head, incidentally not always in perfect register. In recent years however, the printers seem to have discovered a sufficiently fast gold ink, and the heads are once again flat-printed.

Some stamp designs, for example the 'Social Reformers' of 1976, extend to the perforations and beyond (on marginal stamps), with a narrow part of the design appearing in the sheet margins. The extensions are simply trimmed images from the multipositive, surplus to requirements.

Colour shifts attract more attention than most other varieties, but they are very common on photogravure issues and have little significance as errors unless they are very marked with possibly part of the design missing. They are caused by faulty registration of one or more cylinders in the multicolour press, usually seen as an overlap of certain colours and parts of the design. Where two blended colours form part of a design, the shift of one of them will create a 'double' impression. Recorded examples include the liner R.M.S. *Queen Elizabeth 2* (S.G. 778) with two funnels

(instead of one) and an amusing one: the polar explorer Sir James Ross (S.G. 897), whose eyeballs rested on his cheeks. Such varieties are not constant and are generally confined to one sheet.

Another common form of variety is the *doctor blade flaw*, caused by faulty wiping of the surplus ink on the printing cylinder, and generally visible as white or coloured lines extending down or across the sheet of stamps. The doctor blade is a fixed steel blade mounted on a heavy base which moves from side to side across the path of the revolving cylinder, just touching it, as it

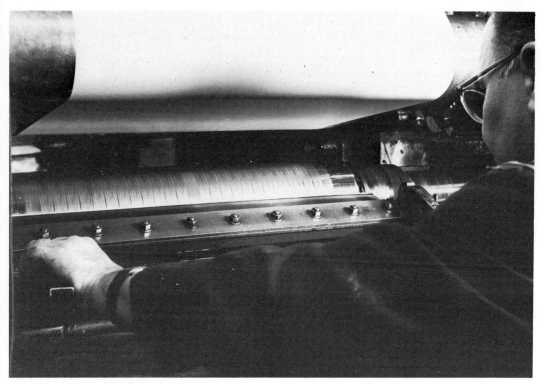

An excellent view of the 'doctor blade' on a modern high-speed photogravure printing press. It can be seen in the centre of the picture, fixed to the frame of the press with a series of large bolts.

scrapes off the superfluous ink. A particle of grit wedged momentarily between the edge of the blade and the surface of the cylinder will leave a 'trail' on the printed stamps, usually a fine hairline which peters out almost at once or possibly after several sheets (in the web) have been printed. The crosswise motion relieves wear and tear on the cylinder, helps to dislodge debris and explains the slight deviation from the vertical or horizontal of the hairline flaws.

Stamp booklets and the rolls of coil stamps used in automatic vending machines are made up from specially printed sheets, the stamps being arranged to provide identical panes of four or six stamps for booklets

Broken shoe of rider on the G.B. $8\frac{1}{2}$p Caxton commemorative of 1976, listed as S.G. 1014 V394.

(with a narrow selvedge for stitching) or to permit splitting and reeling as single-value or multi-value coils. The early coils were adapted from ordinary sheets, though.

As the basic printing process is the same as for ordinary stamps, the booklet and coil stamps have similar varieties to those previously described; constant varieties will usually recur on the same stamp in the pane of a specific booklet, or on every 21st stamp of rolls having vertical delivery in machines (every 25th stamp in sideways-delivery ones). Large, jagged teeth-marks in addition to the perforations on coil stamps are caused by the claws which control the release of the stamps in the machine becoming out of alignment with the roll.

Phosphor bands were applied by photogravure to certain 'Wilding' definitives, to the range of 'Machin' low values including the current issues – two bands for all denominations except that representing the basic second-class rate, which has a single centre band – and to commemorative or special issues from 1965. Since 1972 the latter have been printed with 'all-over' phosphor. The photogravure bands have a 'screened' pattern and do not indent the paper.

Varieties include missing bands (which are listable) and those which are misplaced. Misplaced bands are listed only if two narrow bands appear as one broad band or if a shift on a two-band stamp causes the omission of one of the bands.

Embossed stamps

Embossing or die-stamping was introduced in Great Britain by William Wyon, chief engraver to the Royal Mint (whose head of Queen Victoria for the City Medal of 1837 was the model for all the British stamps of her reign), and by Charles Whiting, a printer, in the form of essays for stamping paper submitted in 1840. In the event, Wyon's embossed head was used for the first embossed envelopes in 1841, while he also prepared the matrix for the G.B. embossed stamps of 1847-54.

Colour shift on the photogravure G.B. 3p 'Churches' stamp of 1972, resulting in a red coat on the doorpost!

The process involved the use of two dies, one cut in deep recess (the 'female'), the other in corresponding relief (the 'male'). From the primary (recessed) die, punches were made in relief and used to produce replicas of the matrix to which were added the engraved octagonal-shaped, engine-turned frames, also the pendant curl at the back of the Queen's head, omitted on the primary die. Again punches were made: these were inscribed with the word POSTAGE and the respective face values, and used to produce the completed working dies used in the embossing presses.

Printing was effected by inking the flat portions of the die, then pressing the paper on to it to obtain the colourless raised impression of the Queen's head. Each impression was stamped singly on the sheet, one at a time, and consequently there was wide variation in the spacing of the stamps; in many instances the design images over-lapped. Varieties occurred in the form of double (or weak) impressions, and when some sheets of the 6d. were printed on the gummed side.

Another classic issue of embossed stamps was the series printed by De La Rue for Gambia from 1869 to 1887. These stamps were separately printed and embossed on letterpress machines, the coloured portions of the stamps – frame and background – being typographed in the normal manner with the Queen's profile left blank. In a separate operation the embossed heads were impressed from a plate formed of plaster of Paris replicas of the original recessed die, used as a matrix. Thus the printed sheets of stamps were literally squeezed between the steel die and the raised image of the plaster matrix.

Varieties of the Gambian embossed issues consist mainly of faulty registration of the embossing in relation to the printing, and this so-called *double embossing* has no special value. Weak impressions may cause the pendant curl at the back of the Queen's hair to be correspondingly weak or missing altogether, while broken letters (being

normal letterpress flaws) may be found in the inscriptions GAMBIA and face values.

The stamps of Heligoland, 1867-76, were typographed with the Queen's head embossed in colourless relief, while the embossed heads of reigning monarchs were a feature of Portuguese stamps from the first issue of 1853 to abqut 1884, where again the consistent varieties were double impressions. Modern stamps are occasionally partially embossed, notably in Austria and Germany, while the numerous independent states and republics of Africa and other parts of the world frequently produce 'gold-plated' stamps, the designs being embossed or die-stamped on gold foil.

3. Varieties of perforation, watermark and paper

Henry Archer's primitive perforating machine, finally accepted in 1852 after his rouletting experiments and first used to perforate G.B. stamps which appeared in January 1854 (1d. red-brown, perf. 16), was the prototype of subsequent comb-perforating machines. Examples and varieties of the experimental and officially-issued Archer-perforated stamps are comparatively rare and keenly sought by collectors. The full details will be found in the Gibbons *Great Britain Specialised* catalogue, volume 1.

With a few exceptions, 14 was the standard gauge for British stamps from 1855 up to and including the issues of King Edward VII; thereafter 15 x 14 (14 x 15 for large vertical-format stamps) became the norm, although the exact gauge varies and is sometimes recorded as $14\frac{1}{2}$ x 14 (or 14 x $14\frac{1}{2}$). Modern stamps are perforated by sheet-fed machines such as the ubiquitous Grover, employing a two-row comb, or by reel-fed machines using a three-row comb. The Kampf rotary perforator built into Harrisons' Jumelle press perforates the stamps as they are printed.

Oddly enough, the rarest form of perforation variety, which nevertheless seems to appear fairly frequently, is the imperforate stamp, occurring in parts of a sheet or even a whole sheet. It is usually the stamps in the top or bottom rows of a sheet in a sheet-fed perforator which miss being perforated due to faulty feeding of the sheets, which miss a strike and slip through the machine. They also sometimes slip through the inspection procedures, to our delight!

British stamps are printed and issued by the million and are thus a prolific source of imperf. and part-perforated varieties. In the various definitive series these occur not only in sheets of stamps, but also in booklets and on the coil stamps obtained from automatic vending machines. Where a single-line perforator is used and a row of perforations is missed the result is a common type of variety known as *imperf. between*, usually a vertical pair which is imperf. horizontally between the stamps. If the vertical pair is also imperforate at top and bottom, indicating that several rows in the sheet were not perforated, such a pair is described as 'Imperf. horiz. (vert. pair)' or, if the vertical rows are imperf., 'Imperf. vert. (horiz. pair)'.

All imperf. varieties are best collected in pairs, or larger multiples if possible, to obviate any suspicion of a 'doctored' single

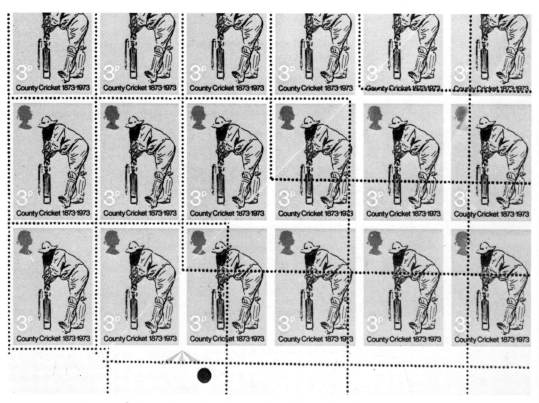

A spectacular mis-perforation on the G.B. 3p 'Cricket' stamp of 1973. The paper fold which caused the error can be seen running diagonally across the centre of the picture.

stamp. A single comb perforator punches three sides of each stamp in a row at a time, thus stamps from an imperforate row will be listed as 'Imperf. three sides (pair)'. Booklet errors listed as 'imperf. panes' show a single row of perforations either at top or bottom of the pane, while 'part perf. panes' have one row of three stamps imperf. on three sides. Part-perforated sheets of the 'Machin' definitives, emanating from Harrisons' Jumelle press, are known to exist.

Wing margins, extra wings or flaps of the margin adjoining the stamps, perforated on the outside, are peculiar to the Victorian era, especially the G.B. surface-printed issues of 1855-83. These were formed when the vertical gutters between panes were perforated centrally instead of close to the divided stamps.

For the student, the various perforation types used in the production of the G.B. Wilding and Machin definitives, the Regionals and the postage dues (sheets and booklets) are given detailed listings in the Appendixes to Volumes 3 and 4 of the Gibbons *Great Britain Specialised* catalogue.

Perforation varieties such as double or misplaced perfs. are not listed in the catalogues as they are usually of a freakish nature, resulting from a mishap to a single sheet of stamps. Some such varieties, however, are quite spectacular as, for example, a shift of paper which results in the perforations running down the middle of of the stamp and across the centre (so that a 'stamp' may comprise four quarters of

Two watermark varieties: left, wrong crown (a St Edward's crown) substituted in Script CA watermark; right, 'Three Roses and a Shamrock'.

different stamps). A sheet of stamps fortuitously folded back as it passes through the perforator can also result in an equally spectacular array of criss-cross perforations across the sheet when unfolded.

Some varieties are due simply to the wrong perforation gauge being utilised for parts of an issue which normally has a certain perforation; these are listed in the main catalogues. The perforation varieties of the early classic issues of the Australian States and New Zealand provide an immense field for philatelic research, while compound, pinhole and 'sewing-machine' perforations, as well as the numerous types of roulette, all contribute to philatelic studies.

Be warned that some stamp booklets are closely guillotined so that the outer edges of the panes of stamps are imperforate. These have no significance, nor do stamps in a sheet with 'blind' or imperfect perforations (holes not punched out). These are due to blunt or missing perforating pins.

Also inconsequential are the misaligned perforations which cause a stamp design to be off-centre, close to the printed design on one side and leaving a wide gap on the opposite side, often with similar aberrations at the top and bottom of the stamp. Sheet-fed perforating machines need (but do not always receive) a watchful eye on the part of the operator. A simple, occasional adjustment is all that is required to maintain perfect registration of the perforator. Stamp-sized, perforated 'blanks' of white paper are simply gutter margins perforated through.

Watermark varieties originate in two

Coil strip of three from Canada, a country whose coil stamps are usually imperf. × perf.

From left to right: normal, inverted and reversed watermarks as
seen from the BACK of the stamps.

From left to right: reversed-and-inverted, sideways and sideways-
inverted watermarks as seen from the BACK of the stamps.

ways: in the course of the manufacture of the paper, or while the stamps are being printed. The watermark is a device or pattern formed (impressed) within the paper by the 'dandy roll' in the wet pulp stage of manufacture. The roller or cylinder has a wire-gauze surface to which are attached the 'bits' – usually emblems in single or multiple form – which are seen as a thinning of the paper.

The first British stamps, and many subsequent issues of both G.B. and the Commonwealth territories (the former colonies), had a single emblem or motif spaced one to a stamp, called a *single watermark* as opposed to a multiple pattern. Occasionally, when a 'bit' became detached, it was either replaced by a slightly different device, replaced inverted or not replaced at all. These mishaps account for some of

the best-known watermark varieties, notably the St. Edward's Crown among the Tudor Crowns on numerous Commonwealth stamps of the 1952-53 era, when a missing crown was replaced by the wrong type. Sometimes the G.B. 'Wilding' definitive issues of the same period are reported with an inverted or missing crown in the Multiple Crowns watermark.

Classic errors of watermark include the 'three roses and a shamrock' (the thistle having been replaced by a rose) in place of the normal emblems on G.B. stamps of 1862-67, and the Transvaal 1d. Edwardian of 1905 with the Cabled Anchor watermark of the Cape of Good Hope instead of the normal Multiple Crown CA.

Inverted watermarks are due, in the main, to single sheets being presented wrong way round in the sheet-fed printing press.

A 'dandy roll' used in the manufacture of watermarked paper.

These, and reversed (or 'back to front') varieties are fairly common, as also are sideways watermarks, and there are various permutations such as inverted *and* reversed, sideways-inverted etc., as seen through the front of the stamp. Remember, however, that some British stamps were normally printed with inverted watermarks for use in stamp booklets, while sideways watermarks appeared on stamps from rolls used in vending machines with sideways delivery, and in certain booklets. Also many modern G.B. stamps exist without watermark due to the misplacement of the paper in printing.

Rowland Hill introduced the Small Crown watermark in his 'Blacks' and 'Blues' as a

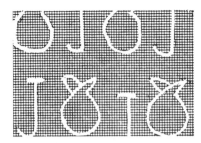

'Multiple J and Pineapple' watermark found on modern Jamaican stamps.

'Multiple Cockerel's Head' watermark used by Malawi.

precaution against forgery; in various forms the watermark has continued in use through the reigns on G.B. and Commonwealth stamps, and in some foreign countries, too. British stamps ceased to have watermarks with the introduction of the 'Machin' definitives in 1967, but numerous Commonwealth territories carry on the old tradition of watermarked stamps. Countries represented by the Crown Agents currently use the diagonally-arranged Multiple Crown CA watermark; others, Jamaica for example (Multiple 'J' and Pineapple), use their own devices.

While the majority of stamps are printed on wove paper, which has a smooth, even texture, numerous other types of paper have been used. These are fully described in the Introduction to the Gibbons *British Commonwealth* catalogue. The first British stamps and other early issues were printed on hand-made paper which varied considerably in thickness. The G.B. 1d. red and 2d. blue stamps from 1841 to 1857 had paper more or less blued, caused by chemical action between the paper and the fugitive printing ink, but the 1d. black on blued (or *bleuté*) paper constitutes a variety.

The so-called *ivory head variety* in which the Queen's head appears white on the back of the aforementioned 1d. reds and 2d. blues (of 1841) was due to a lack of ink – and a corresponding absence of blueing – on the head. The 4d. carmine of 1855-56, Britain's first surface-printed issue, was printed on highly glazed, deeply blued paper; varieties may be found with the paper slightly blued or white. Conversely, the 4d. rose-carmine of 1857, issued on ordinary white paper, exists on the thick glazed paper of previous issues. Thick paper and azure-toned (pale blue) varieties are recorded among the surface-printed issues of 1862-64 and 1865-67.

Stamp papers range from thin and hard to thick and soft, and identification is important in classifying stamps which were successively printed on different kinds of paper, especially the early issues of the Australian States, Canada and New Zealand. Generally, any stamp which differs from the normal in texture or colour, originally issued thus, may rank as a variety.

4. Tools for the Job

Some accessories are essential items of equipment for all stamp collectors, not only variety hunters: tweezers, perforation gauge and watermark detector.

Stamp tweezers are easy to handle with a little practice and they are a necessary aid to sorting loose stamps, placing stamps in a stockbook or mounting stamps in an album. They are available gold, chromium or nickel plated with a choice of medium, broad or spade ends.

Perforation measurements are based on the number of holes within the prescribed length of two centimetres – a little more than $\frac{3}{4}$ inch. The ordinary card, ivorine or plastic gauges are inscribed with rows of dots of varying size (equivalent to the sizes of the perforation holes) within this set measure. When a stamp's perforations are matched to the appropriate row of dots, it is then possible to read off the measurement by the figures quoted at the end of the row. 'Perf. 14' (or 'P 14' in the catalogue) indicates that the stamp is perforated 14 on all four sides, whereas 'Perf. 12 x 14' signifies a compound perforation: 12 at the top and bottom and 14 at the sides.

The *Instanta* perforation gauge employs a continuous scale and provides more accurate measurements to the nearest decimal point. The transparent gauge is laid

'Almost symbolic significance . . . '

Using benzine to show up a Script CA watermark.

over the stamp, aligned with a guide-line on the left and moved forwards or backwards until the converging lines on the gauge correspond exactly with the stamp's perforation holes (or 'teeth'). The measure is indicated by figures on the left and right.

Watermarks are not always easily seen and some form of detection aid is necessary to establish the type of watermark (and a stamp's value), or reveal a variety. The traditional method is the use of a benzine-dropper with a watermark tray the stamp is laid face down in the tray and a few liberal drops of benzine allowed to fall on it when, momentarily, the image of the watermark should be visible. Benzine, however, is highly inflammable and may deface photo-gravure-printed stamps.

A magnifying glass has an almost symbolic significance for the variety collector – never

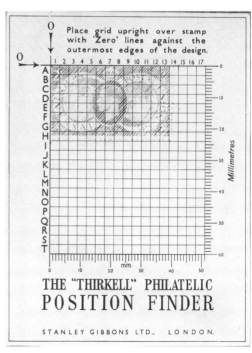

The 'Thirkell' position finder.

be without one! You need a good lens to spot some of the more elusive errors and varieties, and I recommend a small folding magnifier for the pocket, a more powerful reading glass for the desk. Magnification enhances the fine detail of a printed stamp and helps one to identify the different printing processes.

Lastly, there is the *Thirkell* Position Finder, which is in the form of a transparent plastic grid, lettered and numbered, with which one can plot the position of flaws and varieties on stamps for record purposes. Simply placed over the stamp and aligned at top and left, the *Thirkell* indicates the location of the flaw according to the square in which it occurs, expressed as 'D 4' or 'G 6–H 7' etc. A millimetre scale is included.

Index to Varieties Described